FIND YOUR PURPOSE

Based on *The Purpose Handbook* by
Eloise Skinner

First published in Great Britain by Practical Inspiration Publishing, 2026

ISBN 978-1-78860-907-4 (paperback)
978-1-78860-908-1 (ebook)

EU GPSR representative: LOGOS EUROPE, 9 rue Nicolas Poussin, LA ROCHELLE 17000, France Contact@ logoseurope.eu.

Contents

Series introduction

Welcome to *6-Minute Smarts*!

This is a series of very short books with one simple purpose: to introduce you to ideas that can make life and work better, and to give you time and space to think about how those ideas might apply to *your* life and work.

Each book introduces you to ten powerful ideas, but ideas on their own are useless – that's why each idea is followed by self-coaching questions to help you work out the 'so what?' for you in just six minutes of exploratory writing. What's exploratory writing? It's the kind of writing you do just for yourself, fast and free, without worrying what anyone else thinks. It's not just about getting ideas out of your head and onto paper where you can see them; it's about finding new connections and insights as you write. This is where the magic happens.

Whatever you're facing, there's a *6-Minute Smarts* book just for you. And once you've learned how to coach yourself through a new idea, you'll be smarter for life.

Find out more...

Introduction

If someone asked you about your purpose, what would you say?

It seems like such a fundamentally important subject, and yet most of us probably don't have an immediate, clear response. It's possible we spend more time curating our social media feeds than we do our actual existence.

After university, I attempted the typical millennial journey: degree, city career, responsibilities, social life, five-year plan. I always imagined a sense of purpose would fall into place without too much effort. I guess I thought that matching my life up to traditional signs of achievement would reward me with the deeper meaning I'd been looking for. Spoiler alert: it didn't. I felt almost betrayed by this outcome – like I'd been promised something, and when I'd worked to achieve it, it didn't deliver.

And so, I went searching for purpose. I looked for it in job opportunities and charity projects and meditation retreats. I qualified as a yoga teacher and moved to another country. I even spent a year training to be a monk (more on that later). Gradually, I started to gather together purpose-finding practices and tools that, over a long period of time, I used to design a personal sense of purpose, passion and intention.

The beauty of these kinds of purpose-finding practices is that you don't have to become a monk to claim them for yourself. You don't have to spend hours studying, or learn a specific technique, or follow a certain set of rules with perfection. Instead, you can integrate purpose-finding practices into your current life just as it is, bringing with you everything that you have – including the whole of your past, as well as your hopes and dreams for the future. And that's where this book comes in.

The path towards finding your purpose isn't designed to make you into some kind of mission-driven machine, or to give you a singular focus to pursue for the rest of your life. This book is about something much more interesting – the idea that it's possible to experience your life one level deeper than the life you've experienced so far. It's about choosing to create a life infused with intention, integrity and meaning. Fundamentally, this book is centred around the idea that it's possible to *design* the life you actually want to live – to be a creator rather than an observer.

The journey of finding your purpose will, of course, look different for everyone – but this book provides a portfolio of resources to get started. I encourage you to approach the book like a toolkit: full of suggestions and advice, ready for you to try out in practice. See what works; see what doesn't. Add your own suggestions in the margins. Work through it, highlight what you love and revisit it regularly. Take ownership of the process: it's your life, after all.

You might be doing the exercises in this book in 6-minute sprints but remember this is a lifelong journey and there's no finish line; the work is always ongoing. In fact, it might just be the most important work you ever do.

Let's begin!

Day 1
What is purpose, really?

> Purpose: 'The reason for which something is done or created or for which something exists.'

Sounds pretty fundamental, doesn't it? It's a topic that goes to the heart of our existence as humans, but one that's easy to forget beneath the daily chaos of emails, meetings and our ever-expanding to-do lists. It might just be among the most fundamental questions we ever encounter.

The purpose of purpose

It's worth noting that this is not a new question. Although it's often reported that the next generation will demand 'purpose-driven lives', the concept of purpose wasn't invented alongside avocado toast and Instagram. This topic, and the questions that accompany it, have been around for a long time. People have been asking themselves – and each other – about the idea of purpose for thousands of years.

This might remove some of the novelty from the discussion, but it makes it a little more exciting. It means that you're about to become part of a tradition of people who have asked the same questions and who have started to walk the same path. In some ways, the search for purpose connects us to countless numbers of people at a level of depth and continuity that we don't often experience.

At the same time, the question is completely new for each individual, and the work of finding your purpose is utterly unique. In the past, people might have sought purpose through social organizations, family structures or religious communities (and many still do). And, of course, if those paths deliver the structure and the answers you're searching for, that's great. This work can be an addition.

For those of us searching for purpose outside those structures, the same types of 'life questions' are still relevant – this, after all, is the work of being a thinking, feeling human being. Very few people actually do the difficult work of thinking about these life questions in a deliberate, consistent way.

A sense of inner purpose delivers freedom because it can't be taken away by an outside force. It gives you the ability to identify your goals and values, and to choose a path with intention. A strong, grounded sense of purpose also delivers independence; you don't need to enter relationships in order to receive validation or reassurance (whether with other people or with possessions or behaviours).

In terms of the evidence, research has started to show what we've all long suspected: finding purpose in your work life might make you happier, more energized and more fulfilled.[1] So finding (and maintaining) a sense of purpose is a fundamental pillar of wellness; a way to ensure life is lived to its fullest and enjoyed in its highest quality. This could be the journey towards a full, complete human life, and it should be available to everyone. Finding a sense of purpose can change the way you navigate your life, in a very practical sense.

Purpose can become a guide

Life is complex. Throughout your hours on earth, you'll be thrown a multitude of challenges. Those driven by purpose will have a clearer sense of the road ahead. It doesn't guarantee an easy journey, but it can help to keep you on your path. Purpose can operate as a personal compass, pointing you in the right direction when you need to make a decision.

Purpose inspires others

What would it be like if everyone – from your boss to your barista to the tube driver who gets you to work – was driven by a sense of purpose? It would probably be a more energized, more vibrant, more inspired world. The journey to living a purpose-focused life might be slow, but you're likely to carry others with you along the way. Whether you're aware of it or not, you're modelling a purpose-driven lifestyle to everyone you encounter.

Think about your heroes – the people you look up to in your career, or the people who inspire you in your daily life. It's likely that they have at least one thing in common: a resilient sense of who they are and an idea of what they want to contribute to the world. This quality doesn't have to be reserved for heroes and inspirational figures. A purpose-focused life is available to each and every one of us.

Purpose gives rise to grit

Grit – the blend of passion and perseverance that helps you power through the ups, downs, disappointments and difficulties of life – tends to be associated with a clear sense of purpose. And while it might be true that some people are more predisposed to this kind of attitude than others, it can be practised, learned and experienced by anyone.

So what? Over to you…

1. What does 'purpose' mean to you right now, in your own words?

2. Where in your current life do you already see hints of purpose?

3. How comfortable are you with your purpose evolving over time?

Day 2

Why purpose matters, and why now

The work of crafting your life begins here. But there's a question to get to the heart of first: why are we doing this work in the first place? The importance of purpose is not only philosophical – it is deeply practical, and it can change the way you approach everything.

The importance of purpose

Although we don't always choose our circumstances, we are constantly presented with opportunities to interpret events, set goals and develop our own character. Think about all the things that happen to us without our consent – death, illness, global pandemics... But we have the capacity, in any given moment, to decide how to greet the things that come our way. Even in the bleakest scenarios, when the worst possible thing happens, we still have a choice – the choice to respond as we decide.

The skill – and it *is* a skill, which has to be learned – is to identify the gap between stimulus (something happening to you) and response (the way you choose to respond). In that space, you can pause, realign with your purpose and make a decision from that foundation.

How purpose can change the way you live

One famous case is the life of psychologist and psychiatrist Viktor Frankl, who focused his work on the theme of meaning. A long-term prisoner in the concentration camps of Nazi Germany, Frankl endured the loss of his entire immediate family and the brutal inhumanity of life in a camp. His survival, and his enduring belief in the meaning of life, is a testament to the power of purpose.

The heart of Frankl's message is this: no matter the circumstances, we have the capacity to transcend our suffering and rise above it. We have the ability to 'choose our attitude in a given set of circumstances'. The driving force behind this? A sense of meaning. As Nietzsche wrote: 'He who has a why to live can bear almost any how.'[2]

Frankl also observed how the loss of purpose could disempower and even destroy. He recounts the story of an inmate who dreamt he would be liberated from the concentration camps on a specific date. When that date arrived and nothing happened, the man's hope collapsed; he became ill and died soon after. Purpose for him was not a luxury – it was life-sustaining.[3]

These examples may be extreme, but they point to universal truths:

- Each of us has the capacity to choose our response to life
- The will that comes from meaning and purpose can be a powerful source of energy
- Losing that inner drive can change a life's course entirely.

Handling ambition

Talking about purpose and drive naturally leads us to think about ambition – the goals we aspire to. Ambition has a mixed reputation. It can be a gift – we should all feel empowered to use our energy in pursuit of the things we want the most. But it needs to be harnessed effectively. Here are three common problems people face in relation to ambition:

1. **Not ambitious enough.** The first step on the path to finding your purpose is to believe that it's possible to live a purpose-driven life – you don't have to settle for anything less, despite what you might think or believe, or what other people might tell you.
2. **Overly ambitious.** Having high ambitions can be a good thing, but the danger is that you burn out fast or become disappointed when things turn against you. It's also important to cultivate qualities of humility, empathy and self-compassion as a solid foundation to return to when things get difficult. The most powerful tool when it comes to handling your ambition is the knowledge that you always come back to yourself, whether you're successful or unsuccessful in any particular goals you set.
3. **Swinging between extremes.** In some areas of our lives we cultivate high ideals and in others we compromise. It's possible to be both over-ambitious and under-ambitious

about the same thing, sometimes in the same day. One approach is to re-evaluate where your energy is currently going, and (if you feel like it's appropriate) re-orientate it towards goals that are receiving less of your energy and attention. Recalibrating your life like this doesn't have to be dramatic – it can mean simply and slowly redirecting your focus towards new priorities.

The challenges of everyday life

Modern life is hard: full of responsibilities, unexpected and unwanted happenings, and distractions. Even with the best of intentions, it's easy to lose sight of any sense of ultimate purpose among our day-to-day challenges and struggles. We might have many things to be grateful for, yet we're stressed, worried and anxious. We can't sleep properly, or we're burned out, or we're too exhausted to try any more. We've lost sight of what we want to be doing among all the possibilities of what we *could* be doing.

During my time in a monastic community, I noticed that it was much easier to keep sight of the overall goal. Our time was ordered according to a structure of rituals, habits and practices, which all pointed us back towards the overarching 'mission'. It wasn't possible to lose sight of where we were headed because we were consistently checking back in. Let's look more closely at this idea of practice.

The significance of practice

In the monastic community our days had a rhythm to them. Wake up, morning prayer. Breakfast, in silence. Reading, study, tasks around the house and in the garden. Cups of tea. More silence, more tasks around the house, cooking, eating, study. Evening prayer. Sleep.

As the year progressed, I learned more and more about the importance of practice when it comes to the spiritual life. I learned that practice is, in fact, a matter of retraining the patterns of your life to reflect the person you want to be, and the type of life you want to live.

We live in a world of quick fixes, but for every successful person, in every field, there will be an element of consistent, repeated practice.

Purpose-focused work is also a practice; not a one-off event, but something you carry with you. However, it doesn't have to feel like work. I'd encourage you to treat these exercises as an artistic or creative project – something to be carefully considered and treated with integrity; something to be worked on slowly, with intention. And you can't fail at this work. There are no right or wrong answers – just a steady process of discovering yourself.

The search for meaning

Finally, and perhaps most profoundly, let's return to Viktor Frankl. Frankl believed that every human being contains 'spirit' – this wasn't necessarily a religious concept, but more of a universal human element. Within this spirit lies the movement towards meaning. Frankl believed humans have a will to discover this meaning, and that this will could fuel us to endure any suffering to pursue it. So, we are meaning-searching creatures, and the world is open to our interpretation.

Purpose-finding work isn't always comfortable. It often means putting aside the pursuit of pleasure, and there may be some aspects of it that are difficult. It's challenging to get to know yourself on an existential level, and many people choose not to go deeper. But the rewards of the work can be immeasurable, long-lasting and transformational.

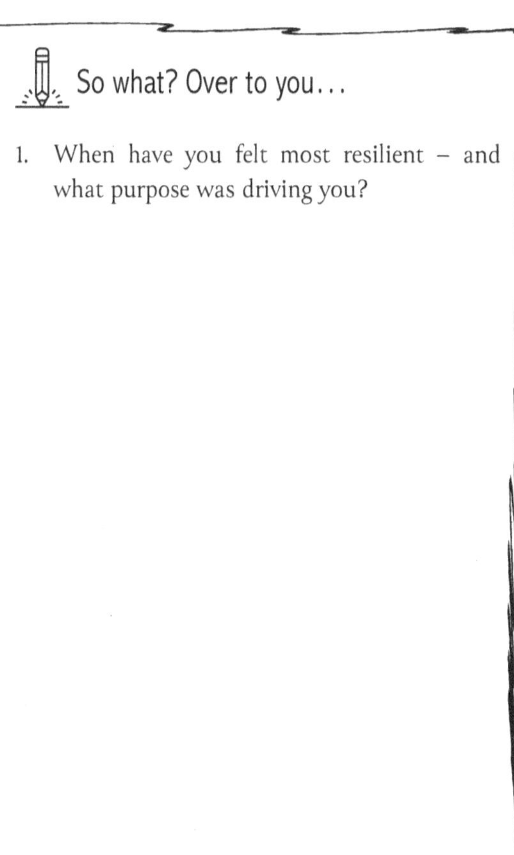

So what? Over to you…

1. When have you felt most resilient – and what purpose was driving you?

2. Where might you need to act on a change you've already noticed?

3. Could you develop a practice around purpose-finding? What would that look like for you?

Day 3
The power of reframing

Perhaps you're convinced on the theoretical benefits of a purpose-driven life. But where to begin? Much of the work of finding your purpose is about discovery, but some of it is also about reframing what's already going on in your life in order to understand it better.

Reframing is about thinking through the reality of your day-to-day existence, to find the depth and direction that exists just beneath the surface. Sometimes, the process of working through purpose-finding exercises will enable you to uncover a deeper sense of purpose that's been there all along.

To get you started on the reframing process, here are a few questions.

1. Who are you helping in the course of your day-to-day life?

Make a list of all the people you help directly: your work clients, your colleagues, your bosses, your family members, your neighbours, your community and so on.

Once you have the list, start to expand it to encompass a broader circle. Consider people you help by contributing to the overall culture of your workplace, or people you help indirectly by volunteering for responsibilities, or by producing new ideas, working on your art or engaging in a process of creativity. Be generous with the boundaries of this exercise. Anything you do to put something useful, positive or beneficial back into the world counts.

Once you have the expanded list, take a long look through it. Is it possible to see a consistent thread between the types of people you help, and the way in which you help them? (There's no need to come up with any revelations at this point – we're just gathering information to help you map out your life in a little more detail.)

2. Does your dream job have an overarching purpose or mission?

Imagine you could work your dream job. What makes that job different from others? Does it have a particular service – or way of delivering a service – that makes it unique? If you're already in a job that suits you well, think about whether your organization has a mission. Does it resonate with you? Does it give you any insight into why you do the work that you do?

3. Can you find pockets of purpose in your existing routines?

Get creative. Even if you don't see your life and work as delivering a sense of purpose (yet), there are nearly always opportunities to spot pockets of purpose for yourself. What about volunteering projects, or mentoring, or creative expression? Sometimes, even a simple chat with a junior colleague or a younger family member can deliver a moment of purpose in an otherwise monotonous day. Again, no need to come to a realization at this point – just note down anything that comes to mind.

After all, we're just getting started.

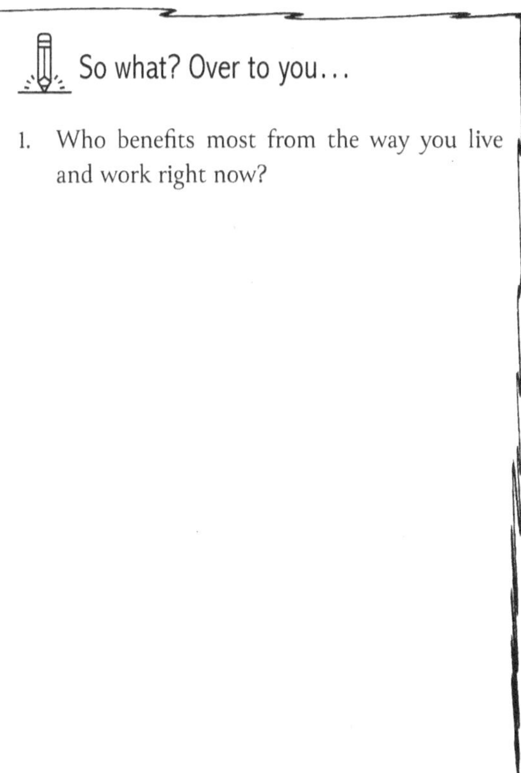

So what? Over to you…

1. Who benefits most from the way you live and work right now?

2. Where could you uncover more meaning in your existing routines?

3. What small reframing shift could you try this week?

Day 4
Purpose vs mission vs passion

You've probably heard the words 'purpose', 'mission' and 'passion' thrown around quite a bit. But what do they actually mean? Understanding their distinctions can give you a clearer framework for shaping your life with intention.

Purpose

Basic definition:

> Purpose is the intention, aim or function of something; the thing something is supposed to achieve.

It's often thought of as 'the thing you're here to do', but your purpose doesn't have to be one fixed idea for life. It's fluid and will (and probably should) evolve over time. At one point your primary purpose might focus on your career. At another, it might centre on relationships, creativity or personal growth. It's OK to let your purpose shift as you develop and progress.

It's also OK if you don't know your purpose yet. Stay curious, be patient, keep asking the questions. Each piece of purpose-focused work is a step on the journey.

Mission

Basic definition:

> A mission is an important goal, accompanied by strong conviction.

Mission and purpose often overlap, but a mission is typically a shorter-term project than your life purpose, and often more specific. You might have several missions running in parallel – one in your work, one in a personal project, another in your family life.

A helpful tool here is the 'personal mission statement'. We'll cover it in depth tomorrow, but for now, think of it as a clear, concise statement of a specific goal and the way you intend to achieve it.

Passion

Basic definition:

> Passion is an intense desire or enthusiasm for something.

Passions can be lifelong or newly discovered. They might relate to hobbies, work, creativity, learning or connection. To uncover them, consider:

- When do you feel most 'in flow' and lose track of time?
- What would you do if money were no object?
- Which activities or topics light you up with curiosity or joy?
- What did you love as a child?

The answers to these questions should give you a sense of where your passions lie – and if you have a long list, you might begin to see consistent themes. They'll probably feed into, or overlap with, your purpose and your mission, too. The intention is for all of these pieces to fit together, giving you greater clarity about who you are and what you might want to do in the world.

So what? Over to you…

1. Which of your passions most influence your current goals?

2. How would you describe your main mission right now?

3. What signs tell you your purpose is shifting?

Day 5

Crafting a personal mission statement

In Day 4, we explored the differences between purpose, mission and passion. Now it's time to put that knowledge into practice by creating a *personal mission statement*. This mission statement is going to be your framework for the road ahead; a place to identify and articulate your most important vision. Here are a few key principles to bear in mind as you approach this exercise.

Three key principles

1. Keep it brief

Aim for a single sentence. You'll explore the details of your mission and values later, but your mission statement itself should be simple and concise. Start long if you need to, then refine until you have the bare framework of your path.

2. Keep it high-level

Your mission statement should be broad enough to adapt with you over time. Compare this exercise to a corporate mission statement – these rarely change dramatically but instead articulate enduring aims. The same applies here: think about the direction you want to maintain five years from now, not just the specifics of today.

3. Make it unique

We're all unique beings, with individual passions and preferences and dreams. But it can be hard to translate that from your inner awareness to a set of words on the page. Resist the temptation to model your mission statement on someone else's – even subtly – especially at the early stages. If you don't feel like your statement accurately reflects the personal qualities and 'essence' of what you want to convey, try stepping away for a while to reflect.

Once you're clear on these principles, you're ready to begin the step-by-step process.

Step 1: Gather your raw material

Make a list of all the things you've valued most from your past, all the things that are most important to you at present, and all the things you want in the world. These three areas (the things you've had, the things you have and the things you want) are a map of your desired past, your present and your future. This is your foundation.

Step 2: Spot the patterns

Review your three lists and look for themes that appear across time. Using a career-focused example, the 'present' column might include your current working environment, and the 'past' column might include previous work experience you've had, but the 'future' column might reflect a different kind of desired career experience. The common theme here might be success, or ambition, or intellectual development.

If you can't find a common theme between your 'past', 'present' and 'future' lists, think about the elements that seem most important to you – which aspects stand out to you as key priorities?

Step 3: Shape the language

Mission statements work best with powerful, assertive language – they should be confident, goal-orientated and bold. Start by writing 'My mission is...' and complete the sentence.

- **Example 1.** My mission is to be an inspiration to my community, and to lead a balanced life.

Here, one focus is external (inspiring others) and the other is internal (self-care). Notice what's not mentioned – career goals, financial targets – this person's priorities lie elsewhere.

- **Example 2.** My mission is to use my natural abilities as a team leader to encourage positive change.

This draws on an acknowledged personal strength (leadership) and ties it to an outward-facing goal. The absence of a focus on relationships or personal wellness aims shows where this person's focus lies for now.

Step 4: Refine and test

Your mission statement will be most useful if you go back to it regularly to refine and revise. Your priorities will change over the course of your life – probably more frequently than you're conscious of – and this mission statement exercise is a great way to stay connected to your path. Revisit it regularly to check it still works for you, and to incorporate any changes you feel are relevant. Keep it somewhere visible (perhaps make it your phone lock-screen or keep it pinned to your wall) so you can continue to check in with it.

A note on flexibility

You should never feel defined or restricted by your mission statement. If you feel you've moved on, review and rewrite it. You can even track your own evolution over the years by seeing how your mission statements change over time.

So what? Over to you…

1. Which patterns appear most clearly in your past, present and future lists?

2. What wording feels both authentic and inspiring for your mission?

3. How will you make sure your mission statement stays in sight – and in use?

Day 6
Self-awareness – the foundation of purpose

A clear, grounded sense of purpose rests on knowing yourself well. In Day 6 we'll explore two practical exercises for enhancing self-understanding.

Exercise 1: The foundational 'why'[4]

In this exercise, you're going to start with a statement beginning with the words: 'I want...'. The statement can relate to anything you like: career, relationship, health or other goals and ambitions. Here are a few examples:

- I want a promotion in the next six months.
- I want to earn [a certain amount of money] by the time I'm 35.

- I want to find a partner and start a family.
- I want to meet all my health and fitness goals by the end of the year.

Once you have your statement, you're going to start unravelling it by repeating the response, 'why?'. If it helps to lay it out in a visual way, you can start with the statement at the top of the page and work down with arrows (similar to a flow-chart). Here's a worked example:

> I want a promotion in the next six months.
> WHY?
> To reach my career goals and develop my professional reputation.
> WHY?
> To feel more comfortable about my career path and know that I'm on the right track.
> WHY?
> To have a general sense of life satisfaction and feel proud of myself for my achievements.

At some point, you can stop the exercise – there'll probably be a natural point where your last 'why' taps into something deep and instinctive, or something that feels like a natural ending to the series of questions. This is sometimes known as your 'foundational why': the 'why' behind all the other 'whys'. But if you reach a final answer that doesn't feel right, you have a couple of options. You can either work back up the chain of 'why' and see if you want to offer a different response to any of the answers you gave. Or you can reconsider your first statement as a whole (i.e. the statement that led to the chain of 'whys') and see if it would be helpful to reassess it.

For example, taking the job promotion example above, if you felt like the final answer (life satisfaction) didn't line up with the initial statement (job promotion), you could use it as an opportunity to rethink. Is there anything else that could deliver life satisfaction in the same way? Is a job promotion really likely to lead to the outcome you want? There are no right or wrong outcomes. The point is just to get to the heart of your life choices.

Exercise 2: One-sentence feedback challenge

In this exercise, you're going to start gathering feedback from other people about what *they* think your purpose is. This is not intended to shape you into the intentions or desires of other people, but just to enable you to formulate a well-rounded view of how you come across in the world. Sometimes, our own perceptions of our lives become so entrenched (and so deeply personal) that it can become difficult to see beyond them. This exercise helps you to take a broader view.

Send a quick message (text or email works well if you don't want to ask in person) to three to five people you trust who know you well but not *too* well – avoid close family members or partners, since you're looking for an objective perspective. You might ask them:

- What was your first impression of me?
- How would you describe me in a single sentence?
- What kind of person do you think I am, if you had to summarize?
- What are my best and worst qualities?
- What do you think I could improve on, as a person?

Don't feel limited to using one of these examples – choose a question you feel will get the most useful response. Keep it short and simple – you could let them know that you're doing a personal development exercise, and you're interested in their thoughts. Mention that you want them to be honest and that they don't have to prepare anything.

When you've collected a few responses, take a look through them. See if there are any consistent themes emerging, or any surprises. Whatever you learn about yourself, try not to be offended. You don't have to accept all feedback as objectively true in order for it to be helpful. Even if you don't agree with an opinion, it still teaches you something about yourself and about your relationship with the other person. This process is all part of knowing yourself (including your friendships, relationships and interactions with others) better.

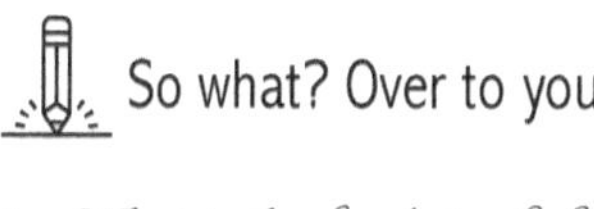

So what? Over to you…

1. What is the *foundational why* behind one major goal right now?

2. What themes emerge when you ask others for feedback?

3. What do you notice as you develop your self-awareness?

Day 7

Telling your story – designing your vision

Whatever you believe about yourself, or about the world, probably comes from some kind of story you've been told. Whether you're spiritual or an atheist, whether you're conservative or liberal, whether you're vegan or not, these are all frequently debated topics, but at the heart of each of them is a story. That doesn't necessarily mean the story is made up. Many of the stories we tell in our society are supported by evidence and backed up by data. But we remember and retain information best when it's presented to us in the form of a story, and over time this story can become our own story: our beliefs, values and principles.

All that is to say... it's important to get the story right. Most people never even think about crafting their own story, but it can be fundamental to designing the life you want. So, this section is an introduction to self-focused storytelling. Who do you want to be? You always get to choose.

We'll approach your story in three stages: past, future and present.

Step 1: Past

The first step is about mapping out your past – from the moment you were born to the moment you're reading this, right now. This is, of course, an immensely complex exercise, but try to keep it light. There are likely to be difficult things, as well as positive experiences, in your past, and it might be helpful to talk them through with someone – a therapist, close friend or family member.

One way to approach this is to identify your defining eras, the phases your life has moved through. A good time period to use for each might be five to seven years (perhaps with a slightly longer period for your childhood years) – you don't have to be too specific. Your eras might look something like this:

0–10: childhood
10–16: early teenage years
16–20: late teenage years
20–28: early adulthood
28–40: adulthood

(and so on – you can design the eras that make the most sense to you).

The idea is just to get a general sense of the phases your life has moved through: an overall 'shape' in your mind, rather than a particular timeline.

Step 2: Future

This is where you record your five-year plan – a map of how you'd like your life to look in five years' time. It doesn't have to be detailed or specific. Think about high-level aspects of life: what you want to be doing with your time, big things you want to have achieved. If you don't have specific goals, you can add more intangible things – for example, the person you want to be in five years, or the qualities you want to develop, or any specific skill-set or abilities you want to gain.

For example:

In five years' time, I want my life to encompass the following:

1. A property that I own.
2. A fulfilling job in my industry that offers me a route to career progression.
3. A creative project (for example, a book) that is long-lasting and that I have worked on over a period of time.

Remember, things change over time, and life will probably take you in an unexpected direction. In some ways, the most *unexciting* outcome would be for all of your plans to perfectly execute themselves without any challenges or hurdles to overcome. Our plans aren't ruined by a change in direction, it just becomes another opportunity to practise agility of thought and creative, strategic responses. So, don't worry if things don't go the way you planned. You *always* get to choose how to respond, and you *always* have an opportunity to redesign your life according to your new circumstances.

Step 3: Present

This step brings us right back to the present. You're going to lay out your past planning (Step 1) and your future planning (Step 2) in one place, then take account of where you are right now.

Record brief responses to the following questions:

1. How do I feel about the journey so far? What are the main thoughts or reflections that I have on my life up to now?
2. What kind of person am I becoming? What have my past experiences and encounters led me to believe about myself and the world?
3. What kind of person do I want to become in the future? Are there any lessons from my past that I want to take forwards, to apply to my future goals and ambitions?

The intention of this exercise is to encourage you to see your life as a story, with you as the main character. The three questions above don't have 'right' answers: you get to choose the qualities that take priority in your life, the kind of person you want to become, the way you feel about what's happened to you so far. You're always in control of the narrative – and if you don't like the outcome of the exercise, start from Step 1 and rewrite it. You are the author of your own existential experience.

Dream CV

Another useful exercise to help you get clear on your vision is to create a 'dream CV'.

First, give yourself 30 minutes to write out your goals. Make them big – outrageous, inspirational, high-level goals. Things you're not sure that you'll ever achieve, that you might never have said out loud. This is an exercise of ambition, of mapping out future desired experiences. Get it all down without judgement, analysis or critical thinking.

Then, start to reshape your goals into tangible, CV-appropriate experiences. This might take a little creative thinking, but there's usually a way to do it for every goal on your list.

For example:

Goal. Have my articles published in major publications (i.e. ones that others have heard of and will recognize).

In this case, in the 'experience' or 'publications' section of your CV template you could add:

Publications. My work has been featured in major publications such as [The New York Times, The Atlantic and The Wall Street Journal]. I am frequently asked to present at conferences and deliver keynote speeches as a result of this work.

It doesn't need to be precise. The point is to transfer your broad, intangible 'dreams' into CV-focused reality. This process of articulation will quickly make clear to you exactly what your dreams might look like, if they came to life. From there, you can work out whether you truly want them or not (this part might surprise you), and if you do, which tiny steps you might put into action to help you get there.

Feel free to leave parts of your dream CV blank or vague – for example, you might replace your job history with a variety of future roles you want to have. You can personalize categories like 'experience', 'awards', 'publications' and so on, accordingly, and you might also find it helpful to design a CV summary or headline that aligns with the person you aspire to be.

The CV exercise is, at its heart, a vision-focused practice. As a result, it's helpful to display your work somewhere it can inspire you. Vision boards are traditionally displayed in a prominent wall space (or, if you're digitally-native, as the background on your laptop or phone). You can do the same with your dream CV – try pinning it to your wall or taking a photo that becomes your background. You should feel free to come back to the CV at any point and revise – it should, ultimately, reflect your current dreams, so if you feel it becomes outdated or you outgrow it, you can return and adjust.

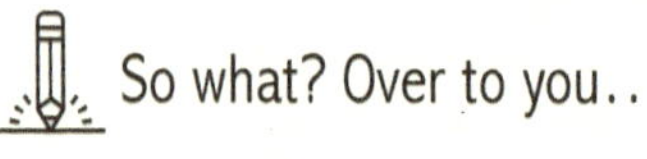

So what? Over to you…

1. What three themes keep reappearing when you map your past, future and present?

2. What do you notice about your dream CV?

3. What have you discovered in this work that surprised you?

Day 8
Creating your rule of life

This is a practice I learned during my time in a monastic community, and it's something that became central to my experience of the year. It's a practice we referred to as 'the rule of life' (the name sounds more dramatic than it is, I promise). The 'rule of life' was essentially a statement of values and principles that we, as members of a community, agreed to shape our lives around. The 'rule of life' title might actually be a little misleading, since it wasn't a strict 'rule' (in the sense that breaking it would have negative consequences). Instead, it was more of an aspirational collection of overarching values that we agreed, as a community, to structure our lives upon.

Here are some (generalized!) examples from our rule of life:

- **Silence.** During times of retreat, periods of silence were structured into our day; in our non-retreat lives, we were encouraged to carve out periods of silence for ourselves.
- **Study and self-development.** We agreed to make study and learning (about ourselves, as well as about theology and philosophy) a central part of our experience.
- **Service with compassion.** We set ourselves the objective to serve each other and people we encountered in the world with compassion, grace and generosity.

You get the idea. These are high-level principles and values that can be applied in a lot of different ways, in a lot of different contexts, over a long period of time. They can also be interpreted differently, depending on the individual applying them. In this exercise, we'll work through how to create your own rule of life.

Take a sheet of paper and start by brainstorming your key personal values and principles, prioritizing your most important ones. Then take a single principle: let's say, for example, generosity. Write the word 'generosity' as your heading and write a short paragraph underneath (three to four lines works best) about the importance of this characteristic and how you intend to uphold it. Here's a worked example.

Generosity:

> Generosity involves giving away my privileges and gifts so that others can benefit. I practise generosity because I understand my connection to others, and I want to use my talents, abilities and opportunities to help where I can. I intend to take every chance to be generous, and I will continually look for ways in which I can give back to others.

Once you've completed one principle, repeat with the others. You're aiming for between seven and ten; not too many that it becomes vague and generalized, but not too few that it becomes overly focused on a singular aspect. Remember, it's your rule of life – make sure you're being honest about the things that matter most to you. Not every principle has to be focused on other people: you can include things like wellbeing, self-care and self-improvement. As with all of the exercises in this book, you're welcome to return to your rule of life at any time and amend or adjust as you feel appropriate.

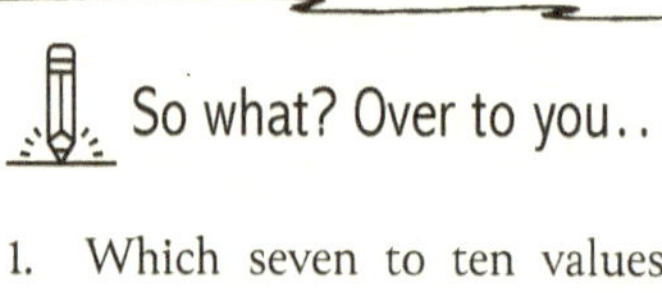

1. Which seven to ten values will form the foundation of your rule of life?

2. How will you translate each value into daily habits or boundaries?

3. Where will you keep your rule so you see and use it regularly?

Day 9

Staying on track – practice and consistency

By now, you're (hopefully!) starting to see a bit of clarity when it comes to figuring out who you are and what you're supposed to be doing with your life. But, as with most meaningful changes, the process of 'finding a sense of purpose' is continually evolving. Today we'll look at how to build your foundations for a purpose-driven lifestyle, setting up habits and practices to keep yourself on the right track as your life – and purpose – develops.

It's *your* life

Let's start with a simple exercise. Take a step into the future (let's say five years from now) and look back at your life in the present moment: your friends, relationships, family members; your home, job and career; your skill-set, goals and ambitions; your body, mind and soul. From that vantage point in the future, how are you feeling about your life at this point, in general? Are you settled? At peace with your past? At home in your body?

The purpose of this exercise, at this point, is not to complete another written reflection, or even to 'discover' anything specifically. It's just to take a quick overview of what you're dealing with, so you can decide which of the activities in this book would fit best into your life and focus on those.

Habit tracking

It's likely you've heard a lot about habits – their power, their utility and their importance in your life. This is a method that encourages you to track them, either to stop or start a habit, or to readjust, re-orientate or realign an existing habit to bring you more in line with your purpose.

You can make a simple habit chart for yourself on a piece of paper (try making a table with the days of the week on the X axis and the number of times a certain habit is repeated on the Y axis), or there are a number of great habit-tracking apps out there that might suit you better.

Once you've chosen your way of tracking, decide how many habits to track and which kinds of habits. In some ways, our whole lives comprise small habits, so be specific about the ones you want to observe or amend. I'd recommend starting with no more than five habits to track (you can always work your way up to a higher number if it turns out to be an effective method for you). Some good examples include:

- Meditation practice
- Drinking water
- Stretching or exercise
- Journalling
- Gratitude practices
- Communication (for example, reaching out to friends, family or networks)
- Giving someone a compliment
- Working on a passion project
- Moments of silence
- Taking a walk outside.

If you wanted to subdivide further, creating categories of items to track, you could split it into:

- Mind
- Body
- Self
- Work
- Other.

Of course, you should personalize and recategorize as you see fit.

The purpose pause

This is a simple daily practice to bring you back into the present moment. Hopefully, the tools we've already explored have given you a sense of what you want to do with your life: the things that matter to you and where you want to be directing your energy. But even with the best of intentions, we can so easily get swept up in the demands of daily life. Sometimes it feels like we take our eye off the ball for a few seconds and wake up a few years later, wondering what exactly it was that we did with our time.

So this practice, while simple, is actually an act of rebellion. It's a push-back against the steady acceleration of culture, both in our working and personal lives. It's a way to reconnect, and you can carry it with you and deploy it at any time. Here are the steps.

Step 1: Notice

This is always the first step in an awareness or meditation-based practice: the simple act of noticing what's going on. Sometimes we catch ourselves on the wrong path – maybe we notice we've been scrolling pointlessly for a while, or we've diverted our attention away from our goal by accident – and we're annoyed about it. The annoyance – though understandable – is misplaced. This is because the noticing (the moment of awareness) is actually the key to returning to your path.

Our whole lives are an ebb and flow of movement. We lean into certain things, we orient our paths in a certain way, and then we forget and fall off track. We decide to start again but slip back into old habits. We have a few weeks off. We return with a new focus. Whenever I work with meditation students, I try to encourage them to lean into this pattern. Instead of fighting to remain in a place of perfection, find the value in noticing when you came off track. The noticing element is helpful, not something to be handled with hostility. The first step is always noticing, and the choice of response can follow.

Step 2: Move your environment

Sometimes the physical shifting of environment can have a profound impact on our internal thoughts, feelings and emotions. Try moving to another room of your house or even stand up and stretch. If you find it effective, you can have a brief clean-up of your desk or your working environment. There's a reason that new starts often accompany a new image or a change of scene – we're visual creatures, and a change of environment often encourages a change on a deeper level of the psyche.

Step 3: Bring your awareness into your body

A simple way to do this is to ground both of your feet on the floor and focus all of your awareness and attention into the soles of your feet. An alternative option might be to place one hand on your heart centre and the other on your abdomen, with the palms facing inwards. A third option might be to place your hands on your knees or thighs with the palms facing down. If you take either of the last two options, think about bringing your attention or awareness to the palms of your hands. Then, run through a quick checklist of questions:

1. How do I feel in my body, right now?
2. How do I feel emotionally, right now?
3. How do I feel in my mind, right now?

The 'emotionally'-focused question is a good one to fit in between body and mind, because it often bridges the gap between the two: emotions might originate in the mind and manifest in the body, or the other way round. It's also helpful to begin this practice with a body focus first because it's often (although not always) easier to sense feelings on a physical level than it is to untangle the layers of thoughts in our minds.

If you don't get any specific answers to the questions, that's fine – at this stage, we're just doing a general check-in. The whole step should only take a few minutes. If you're finding there's more to explore, you can always extend the practice into a longer, body-focused meditation.

Step 4: Tie it back to purpose

Bring yourself back to your purpose in this moment. This might mean refocusing your attention on the task at hand, or it might mean reconnecting with your body, or anything else that feels like it's your purpose in the next hour or so of your day. This practice might give rise to a thought (for example, a reminder that you need to call someone or follow up on a task) – you can always make a quick note of that and then return to this place of pause.

To focus your attention, you can ask yourself the question: 'What is purposeful for me, right now?', or, more straightforwardly, 'What is my purpose in this moment?'

This is, in some ways, a mini-meditation, so it might help to keep your eyes closed (if that feels comfortable), or deepen your breath, or integrate another meditative technique that helps you to focus. But you might prefer instead to make it more of a personal development exercise – maybe make a few notes about your experience or use the moment of 'pause' to organize your materials for the next task on your list. It will probably be the case that different times of your life and your day will require different techniques. As with all of the exercises in this book, the most important thing is that they work to fit you (and not the other way around).

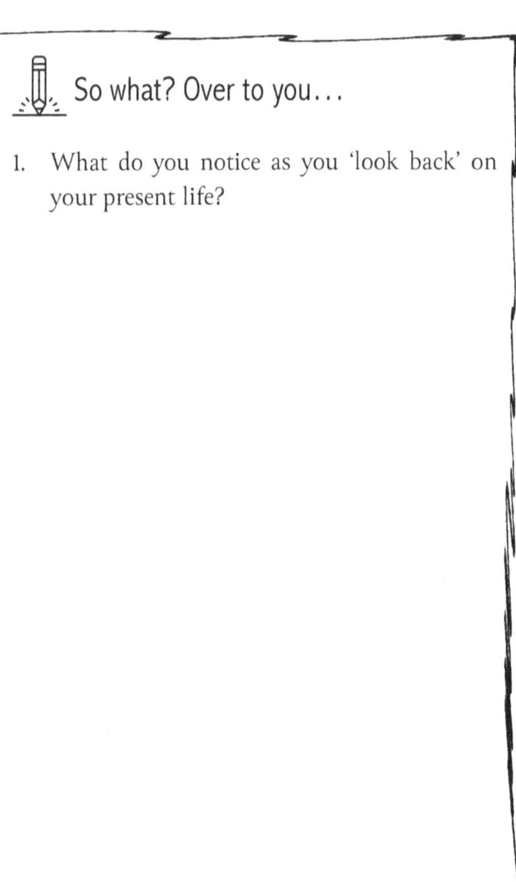

So what? Over to you…

1. What do you notice as you 'look back' on your present life?

2. What new habit would help you to live your purpose?

3. When can you try out a purpose pause this week?

Day 10

Purpose in action – giving back and looking forward

Living with purpose is not only a personal privilege – it carries with it a responsibility. The work you've done to discover your own direction can ripple outward, inspiring and supporting others in their own journeys.

A note on privilege

Purpose-finding work is, in some respects, a privilege to undertake. Most people don't get an opportunity to really analyse and structure their lives in the very deliberate, careful, thoughtful way that you – as a reader of this book – are adopting. Sometimes this is because of the cultural or social context; in other cases it's because of a lack of time, resources or awareness. Sometimes it's even the case that having a comfortable, settled lifestyle can mean that this work isn't necessary. A lot of people move through life without feeling the call to specifically search for their purpose.

I'm assuming, if you've picked up this book and read this far, that you probably don't fall into any of the categories above. You're probably someone (like me) who is a little existentially restless, or someone who is searching for direction. Before you read on, then, just take a moment to appreciate that this is actually a position of privilege. It's a gift to be able to look at your life in detail and make changes where you can. It's a gift to be struggling with these questions, even if they feel difficult and exhausting and confusing. It's a gift that not everyone gets to experience.

There are two important points here: appreciation and giving back.

Appreciation

The first – appreciation – is straightforward. As you progress through this work, see if you can approach it from a position of gratitude. To even get to be doing this work means that you're alive, you're fully awake, you're ready to shape and form and participate in your life. You're living, not just existing.

Giving back

The second – giving back – is a longer-term project. This means that, whenever you get the opportunity to talk to other people about their purpose, or whenever you mentor, supervise or instruct people with less experience than you, you start to give this work back.

This can be in the subtlest of ways – you can talk about your own purpose-finding journey, or you can recommend books (maybe even this one!), podcasts or other resources. Remember that – just like you – people will come to their own purpose-finding journey when they're ready, so don't force it on anyone. But sharing your progress (and your failures and struggles, as well as your successes) can be inspiration for others to begin.

A few final thoughts

Boundaries

One of the most helpful practices for organizing my life purposefully has been boundaries. Boundaries can give you structure and form: they let other people know when it's OK to step closer and when it's not. They can also mark out periods of time – boundaries around your focused working hours; boundaries around your periods of rest and play; boundaries around the things that matter most to you – so you can make sure they're protected.

It's difficult to set boundaries for a variety of reasons. People may not recognize or respect your boundaries (this might especially be the case with close friends or family members, and especially if setting boundaries is new for you). And in a work environment, you might not have much choice about where your boundaries fall (for example, if you're in a junior role).

My hope is that you can use the principles of this book and apply them to boundary-setting. If you can gather information from your purpose-finding work so far, you can make informed decisions about boundaries when it comes to your career or your work in the world. Armed with a clearer vision of what really matters, you can start to decide: where should I allocate my time? What should get priority, and when? How should I choose to structure my life, despite the various demands that are placed on me?

Boundaries can be temporary; if you feel like you need space, claim it for yourself. Open communication and empathy towards other people's feelings is helpful here, too – but remember that the primary purpose of your boundaries is to protect you on a personal level, so maintain the position that makes you feel most safe.

Balance

I don't know if a perfect 'life' balance exists. Instead, I like to think of it as 'integration' – the inextricable blend of your work and your life and your passions and your networks and your wellbeing and your purpose. Integration is everything all wrapped up into one vibrant, complex creation. Go towards the things you care most about; the people you want to keep around; the places you feel at home in; the body and the mental space you know reflects your idea of wellness. Go towards the life you want to design – intentional architecture, based on a lifetime of experience. You get to choose, after all – so you can decide what balance is for yourself.

Being human

One final note to finish our work here. We're probably not getting any of this right on the first try. In fact, there's no idea of 'right' that we're aiming to reach anyway. Instead, we're on a slow mission to become more fully alive, and to redesign our lives around the purpose we're figuring out for ourselves. I'm not sure if we ever really need to find a final, perfect answer – the journey is really the point.

If you've got this far, I'm hoping you'll understand that this book is not intended to give you the answers. Instead, it's a starting point – a map and a guide and a compass to point you in the right direction.

The rest? Well, that's yours to design.

So what? Over to you…

1. How can you give back purposefully, in small or large ways?

2. What boundaries might you need to put in place to protect the work that matters most?

3. What's one step you can take this month to commit to living more purposefully?

Conclusion

Over the last ten days, you've explored your values, your strengths and your 'foundational why'. You've built a vision for your future, created a rule of life and considered how to keep your purpose alive through practice and consistency. You've also reflected on how to give back, sharing your purpose with others in ways that create positive ripple effects.

These are tools you can return to whenever you feel stuck, restless or in need of direction. You might revisit your mission statement every six months, review your rule of life annually or repeat the self-awareness exercises whenever you notice a shift in your priorities.

How purpose can evolve over time

We are complex beings, which means it's not always possible to predict exactly how we'll respond to changes. We're also integrated beings; one part of our life can affect all the others. That means it's hard to isolate parts of our life and address them separately. Purpose-finding work, like everything else, affects everything else.

And finally, we're also constantly evolving beings. You're not the same person you were yesterday, and neither am I. Your values shift, your perspective broadens. Your purpose-finding work should evolve with you.

The key is awareness: noticing when your life is shifting and how you're developing and responding with intention. Many people get stuck along the way; they might start off by following a path that seemed like the right one and wake up a decade later realizing that they never did the continuous work of questioning if it was still the right path. Awareness practices – journalling, reflection, conversations, creative work, meditation, physical activity – can help you notice when change is needed.

Awareness is only the first step – it's another (more challenging) thing to decide to act on that awareness. Taking action takes courage, commitment and maturity. It might mean closing the door on one chapter in order to open another one. It might mean saying goodbye to people, projects and plans that no longer align with where you're headed. It's difficult work, and not everyone wants to do it. But sometimes the consequences of not taking action are even worse: you remain in the same place, unable to respond to the direction in which your life is leading you.

It's your life, after all – it's worth taking the time to shape it with intention.

Endnotes

[1] For example: www.mckinsey.com/capabilities/people-and-organizational-performance/our-insights/help-your-employees-find-purpose-or-watch-them-leave

[2] V. Frankl *Man's Search for Meaning* (1946).

[3] V. Frankl *Yes to Life* (2019).

[4] Sometimes also known as the 'Five Why Method'. See: https://en.wikipedia.org/wiki/Five_whys

Enjoyed this? Then you'll love...

The Purpose Handbook by Eloise Skinner

It's Monday morning, 9am. How do you feel?

Imagine waking up to start another week. In a perfect world, how would you like to feel? Maybe you imagine feeling motivated and energized. Maybe you imagine starting your week with a sense of purpose, peace and intention.

The goal of this book is simple: to help you live with a sense of purpose. Part-manual, part-manifesto, this book is not a quick fix for happiness; it's not a five-day plan promising a fast result. Instead, it's a companion, your personal guide to navigating your own sense of purpose as it evolves throughout your life.

Eloise Skinner is an author, therapist and teacher. She's also the founder of The Purpose Workshop, an agency helping clients to navigate their purpose and redesign their lives.

Eloise studied at Cambridge, trained at Oxford and practised as a corporate lawyer, but after some soul-searching (including a year training to be a monk!) she followed her passion into psychotherapy.

Above all, Eloise is driven by the idea of integration – the power of bringing together all aspects of work and life; to live fully, with intention, integrity and purpose.

Other *6-Minute Smarts* titles

Beating Burnout (based on *The Burnout Bible* by Rachel Philpotts)

Building Great Teams (based on *Workshop Culture* by Alison Coward)

Collaborate Better (based on *Collabor(h)ate* by Deb Mashek PhD)

Customer Success Essentials (based on *The Customer Success Pioneer* by Kellie Lucas)

Do Change Better (based on *How to be a Change Superhero* by Lucinda Carney)

Find Your Confidence (based on *Coach Yourself Confident* by Julie Smith)

Get That Promotion (based on *Getting On* by Joanna Gaudoin)

Grow Your Product Business (based on *Tame Your Tiger* by Catherine Erdly)

How to be Happy at Work (based on *My Job Isn't Working!* by Michael Brown)

How to Get to Know Your Customer (based on *Do Penguins Eat Peaches?* by Katie Tucker)

The Inclusion Mindset (based on *Beyond Discomfort* by Nadia Nagamootoo)

The Listening Leader (based on *The Listening Shift* by Janie Van Hool)

Love Your Job (based on *WorkJoy* by Beth Stallwood)

Managing Big Teams (based on *Big Teams* by Tony Llewellyn)

Mastering People Management (based on *Mission: To Manage* by Marianne Page)

No-Fluff Soft Skills (based on *Soft Skills, Hard Results* by Anne Taylor)

No Nonsense PR (based on *Hype Yourself* by Lucy Werner)

Present Like a Pro (based on *Executive Presentations* by Jacqui Harper)

Reimagine Your Career (based on *Work/ Life Flywheel* by Ollie Henderson)

Sales Made Simple (based on *More Sales Please* by Sara Nasser Dalrymple)

The Speed Storytelling Toolkit (based on *Exposure* by Felicity Cowie)

Stay Focused (based on *Attention!* by Rob Hatch)

Write to Think (based on *Exploratory Writing* by Alison Jones)

Look out for more titles coming soon! Visit www.practicalinspiration.com for all our latest titles.

www.ingramcontent.com/pod-product-compliance
Lightning Source LLC
LaVergne TN
LVHW051014080826
845145LV00009B/2623